On the Go
Diggers

David and Penny Glover

WAYLAND

First published in 2007 by Wayland

Copyright © Wayland 2007

Wayland
338 Euston Road
London NW1 3BH

Wayland
Level 17/207 Kent Street
Sydney, NSW 2000

Editor: Camilla Lloyd
Editorial Assistant: Katie Powell
Designer: Elaine Wilkinson
Picture Researcher: Kathy Lockley

Picture Acknowledgements: The author and publisher would like
to thank the following for allowing these pictures to be reproduced in
this publication: Cover: JCB and Volvo (inset); JCB: 2, 5, 6, 7, 11t, 13, 14,
16, 17, 20; Terex GmbH: 19; Volvo: 1, 4, 9, 18; Gunter Marx/Alamy: 10,
AdrianSherrett/Alamy: 15; CP Stock/Constructionphotography.com: 8,
12; Charles O' Rear/Corbis: 11b, Michael Pole/Corbis: 21, Corbis: 22.

With special thanks to JCB, Terex GmbH and Volvo.

British Library Cataloguing in Publication Data
Glover, David, 1953 Sept. 4-
        Diggers. - (On the go)
        1. Excavating machinery - Juvenile literature
        I. Title II. Glover, Penny
        629.2'25

ISBN-13: 978 0 7502 5069 6

Printed in China

Wayland is a division of Hachette Children's Books

Contents

What are diggers?

Diggers are big digging machines.
Diggers dig deep holes and long
trenches. This digger is digging
a trench for a new pipe.

digger

trench

digger arm

rubbish

skip

Sometimes diggers pick things up. This digger is putting rubbish in a skip.

Digger quiz
Why is the digger digging a trench?

Digger parts

cab

boom

bucket

The digger driver sits in the **cab**. This is high up so he can see all around. The digger's arm is called a **boom**. It swings and bends to move the **bucket**.

teeth

The bucket is on the end of the boom. It scoops up soil and rocks. The bucket has sharp teeth to cut through the ground.

Digger quiz

Where is the digger's bucket?

How does it work?

joystick

The driver uses **levers** called **joysticks** to make the digger work.

The driver can turn the boom and the bucket to pick up a **load**.

8

The boom bends
to move the load
up and down.
It has a
special **joint**,
like an elbow.
The bucket tips
to empty its load.

joint

Digger quiz

How does the driver
work the digger?

Tracks and wheels

tyre

wheel

Some diggers move around on wheels.

A rod called an **axle** fixes the wheels to the digger's body. The wheels have thick rubber tyres to grip the ground.

tracks

links

Some diggers move around on **tracks**. Each track is a loop of metal links. Tracks help the digger to grip the ground and stop it slipping.

Digger quiz
How are wheels fixed to a digger's body?

What makes it go?

fuel tank

The digger's **engine** makes it go. The engine turns the wheels or tracks to drive the digger along.

The engine runs on **diesel fuel**. The driver fills up the tank to make the engine work.

The engine powers the boom and bucket too. The joint bends and special **pistons** make the parts move.

joint

piston

Digger quiz
What kind of fuel does a digger use?

Special jobs

Diggers move rocks and rubble to build new roads. This digger has a **drill** to make holes for posts or to plant a tree.

drill

The scrapyard digger has a **grapple** instead of a bucket. The grapple grips like a hand to pick up metal.

grapple

Digger quiz
Where can a digger use a grapple?

Mini diggers

A big digger cannot fit inside a house but a mini digger can. A mini digger works just like a big digger but it has a smaller bucket and boom.

It's hard work to dig a pond with a spade. A mini digger soon gets the job done.

Digger quiz
What can a mini digger do?

Giant diggers

Giant diggers work in **quarries**, digging up rocks. The digger breaks the rocks with its bucket. Its teeth are bigger and stronger than a dinosaur's.

The RH400 is the biggest digger in the world. The RH400 is so big it has beds and a bathroom inside.

Digger quiz
How does a giant digger break up rocks?

Digging safely

Diggers are very powerful machines. You must never go near a digger when it is working. A safety fence keeps people away from danger.

safety fence

Diggers make lots of noise.
Drivers wear muffs to protect
their ears. They always wear hard
hats, just in case a loose stone hits
their head.

Digger quiz
**Why does the driver
wear a hard hat?**

Old Diggers

steam digger

The first diggers used steam to move.
Before diggers were invented people
had to dig everything with spades.
This **steam digger** loads rock onto
the train.

Digger words

axle
The rod through the centre of a wheel.

boom
The digger's arm.

bucket
The heavy scoop on the end of the boom. The bucket has sharp teeth to cut into soil or rock.

cab
The part of the digger in which the driver sits.

diesel
The fuel a digger engine uses to make it go.

drill
A tool that turns to make a hole.

engine
The part of the digger that makes it work.

fuel
Something that burns inside an engine to make it work.

grapple
A tool made of large spikes that can pick up pieces of metal.

joint
The part of the digger's boom that bends so that it can move the load up and down.

joystick
A lever that works the boom or bucket.

lever
A control like a stick that you move to make something work.

load
Something you lift or carry.

piston
The rod attached to the boom's joint. It makes the boom and the bucket move.

quarry
A place where rocks are dug up from the ground.

steam digger
An old fashioned digger powered by steam.

track
The metal links that some diggers move around on instead of wheels.

trench
A long narrow hole in the ground.

Quiz answers

Page 5 For a new pipe.

Page 7 On the end of the boom.

Page 9 With joysticks.

Page 11 With axles.

Page 13 Diesel fuel.

Page 15 In a scrapyard.

Page 17 Fit inside a house and dig a pond.

Page 19 With its bucket.

Page 21 In case a loose stone hits his head.

Index